GARTER SNAKES

DOUG WECHSLER

ACADEMY OF NATURAL SCIENCES

The Rosen Publishing Group's
PowerKids Press™
New York

For Debbie, with my love

About the Author
Wildlife biologist, ornithologist, and photographer Doug Wechsler has studied birds, snakes, frogs, and other wildlife around the world. Doug Wechsler works at The Academy of Natural Sciences of Philadelphia, a natural history museum. As part of his job, he travels to rain forests and remote parts of the world to take pictures of birds. He has taken part in expeditions to Ecuador, the Philippines, Borneo, Cuba, Cameroon, and many other countries.

Published in 2001 by The Rosen Publishing Group, Inc.
29 East 21st Street, New York, NY 10010

First Edition

Book Design: Michael de Guzman

Photo Credits: pp. 4, 7, 11, 16, 19, 20, 22 © Doug Wechsler; pp. 8, 15 © Breck P. Kent/Animals Animals; p. 12 © Zigmund Leszczynski/Animals Animals.

Wechsler, Doug.
    Garter snakes / Doug Wechsler.— 1st ed.
      p. cm.— (The really wild life of snakes)
    Includes bibliographical references (p.).
    Summary: Briefly describes the physical characteristics, behavior, and habitat of garter snakes, along with some interesting facts about these snakes.
    ISBN 0-8239-5601-6 (alk. paper)
    1. Garter snakes—Juvenile literature. [1. Garter snakes. 2. Snakes.] I. Title.

QL666.0636 W43 2000
597.96'2—dc21   00-023746

Manufactured in the United States of America

CONTENTS

385

HOW THE GARTER SNAKE GOT ITS NAME

A dark snake with three long yellow stripes on its back slithers through the violets in the garden. Between the stripes it has a checkerboard pattern. This is one of the most familiar snakes in North America. It is a garter snake. The garter snake got its name from the **garters** that some men wore to hold up their socks. The garters were brightly colored just like the stripes on the snakes. Not all garter snakes have yellow stripes. Some have red, orange, blue, or green stripes. A few have no stripes at all.

A garter snake is easily recognized by the three long yellow stripes that run along the length of its body. Its name comes from this garterlike pattern.

GARTER SNAKES, LONG AND SHORT

There are 30 **species** of garter snakes. They live from the middle of Canada to Costa Rica in Central America. The longest garter snake is the giant garter snake. It grows up to 5 1/2 feet (1.7 m) long. The smallest garter snake is the adult short-headed garter snake. It is about 16 inches (40.7 cm) long. The short-headed garter snake lives only in a small part of western Pennsylvania and western New York. The most familiar garter snake is the common garter snake. It is found all across southern Canada and in all but the driest parts of the United States. Another garter snake that is widely seen is the ribbon snake. Ribbon snakes are long, skinny garter snakes that are usually found near water.

This eastern ribbon snake is at home in the dry bed of a pond. Garter snakes can be found in a variety of places, such as rocky hills and swamps.

WHAT'S FOR DINNER?

Common garter snakes eat many types of foods. Babies feed on worms and **leeches**. As they grow, they start to eat fish, tadpoles, and frogs. Some of the largest common garter snakes eat mostly meadow mice.

Some garter snakes eat only a few kinds of foods. For example, the short-headed garter snake eats nothing but earthworms. The northwestern garter snake dines on **slugs** and worms. Giant garter snakes and ribbon snakes live in and near water and eat fish and frogs.

Worms are a favorite food of small garter snakes. Larger garter snakes eat frogs, fish, and sometimes even mice.

A baby garter snake looks fierce as it opens its mouth wide to bite a worm. It pulls the worm toward its body and swallows it. A minute later the worm is gone and the snake is fatter. Garter snakes that eat fish need to learn to grab the fish by the head. It is very hard to swallow a fish tail first. Garter snakes grab fish from the surface of the water or underwater. A large garter snake grabs a mouse with its teeth. The snake then loops its body around the mouse to hold on to it. The **venom** in the snake's **saliva** slows the mouse down as the snake starts to eat it for dinner.

A garter snake hunting for fish or frogs flicks its tongue as it swims along the shore. When it finds food, it grabs it with its mouth.

DOUG SAYS

WHEN A GARTER SNAKE BITES, ITS SALIVA CAN PRODUCE SWELLING OR A BURNING RASH IN SOME PEOPLE (1 IN 100).

HIBERNATING

Snakes that live where the winters are cold have to **hibernate**. Garter snakes often hibernate together in **dens**. The den might be a small cave, a pile of rocks covered with soil, or a well. The den must stay above freezing **temperature** or the snakes will die. The snakes also have to stay cool. When a snake is cool it uses less energy. By spending the winter in a cool den, garter snakes have plenty of energy when they come out in the spring.

The most amazing garter snake dens are in Manitoba, Canada. There, thousands of garter snakes spend the winter together in small caves. On the first few warm spring days, there are so many snakes outside the den that they look like a big helping of dark spaghetti.

On an early spring day, garter snakes come out from their den after hibernating all winter. They gather in the warm sun, looking like a serving of dark spaghetti.

◀

MATE AND MIGRATE

Male garter snakes come out of the den first. When the females come out, the males crowd around to **mate** with them. After a female mates with one of the males she leaves the den. She travels to her feeding area for the summer. Later the males also **migrate** to their feeding areas. These areas can be up to 11 miles (17.7 km) away from the den.

The young are born far from the den. How do they find the den in the fall? They follow the scent trail left behind by other garter snakes that know the way. They flick their tongues to pick up the scent.

A female garter snake gives birth to many babies. Baby garter snakes are born live, not hatched from eggs. Mother garter snakes can have from 6 to over 30 baby snakes at a time.

DOUG SAYS

GARTER SNAKES CAN
GIVE BIRTH TO OVER 30
YOUNG AT ONCE.
BETWEEN 10 AND 15 IS
THE USUAL NUMBER.

GARTER SNAKES ON THE MENU

The life of a garter snake is full of danger. Hawks, crows, raccoons, and some types of fish are just a few of the **predators** that eat garter snakes. We could fill this whole page with a list of all their predators. Baby garter snakes are the size of a large worm. Most animals that eat worms would be just as happy to eat a little snake. **Shrews**, frogs, Pacific giant **salamanders**, and even diving beetles find garter snakes very tasty. Sometimes the tables turn as the garter snake gets older. Bullfrogs eat small to medium sized garter snakes, but big garter snakes eat small to medium sized bullfrogs.

This young ribbon snake needs to be on guard for its enemies, such as crows, who will try to eat it.

SMELLY DEFENSE

How does a garter snake protect itself from its enemies? The first thing a garter snake will do is try to escape. As it slides away, its stripes confuse the enemy. The stripes on a moving snake make it hard for the enemy to tell what part of the snake is the tail and what part is the head. If the snake is cornered, it will hold its neck in an "S" shape and open its mouth. Then it will strike at the enemy. What happens when you catch a garter snake? The snake will smear your hand with poop mixed with a special nonpoisonous but smelly liquid. This liquid comes from **glands** near the beginning of the tail.

A garter snake is getting ready to strike its enemy. Its neck is held in an "S" shape and its mouth is open.

DOUG SAYS

I DON'T MIND THE SMELL WHEN I CATCH A GARTER SNAKE, BUT FOR SOME REASON NOBODY WANTS TO BE NEAR ME AFTERWARD.

GROWING AND SHEDDING

When a garter snake is born, it comes out of the mother **coiled** up in a tiny clear **sac**. Minutes later it breaks out of the sac. The smallest garter snake species are almost five inches (12.7 cm) long at birth. The largest species are about 10 inches (25.4 cm) long. As the snake grows, it sheds its skin. The snake grows a new layer of skin beneath the old one. The old skin loosens from the new one. Then the snake moves its jaws and its head out of the old skin. It crawls out of the old skin and leaves it in one long piece. Young snakes may shed their skins several times each year.

A garter snake sheds its skin. The old skin loosens from a new layer of skin growing underneath it. The snake crawls out of the old layer, leaving it in one long piece.

WHERE TO FIND GARTER SNAKES

Many species of garter snakes are common in most of the United States and southern Canada. The best places to look for them are near streams, in wet meadows, and in fields. Garter snakes like to have some sun, so dark forests are not good places to look. They like water, too, so you will not find them in deserts without streams. Garter snakes often rest under boards and flat rocks. Do not lift boards and rocks with your fingers if poisonous snakes also live in the area. Garter snakes may try to bite, but they usually calm down if handled gently. Garter snakes are harmless to humans.

GLOSSARY

coiled (KOYLD) Wound into a ring.

dens (DENZ) Underground places where snakes spend the winter together.

garters (GAR-ters) Bands or straps that hold up socks.

glands (GLANDZ) Organs that make and give out a certain substance.

hibernate (HY-bur-nayt) To spend the winter in a deep sleep.

leeches (LEE-chuz) Wormlike animals that live in the water and feed off of other animals' blood.

mate (MAYT) When a male and female join together to make babies.

migrate (MY-grayt) When large groups of birds, animals, or people regularly move from one place to another.

predators (PREH-duh-ters) Animals that kill other animals for food.

sac (SAK) A pouchlike part in a plant or animal.

salamanders (SA-luh-man-durs) Amphibians that resemble a lizard but breathe through gills and do not have scaly skin.

saliva (suh-LY-vuh) The liquid in the mouth that starts to break down food and also helps food slide down the throat.

shrews (SHROOS) Tiny mouselike animals that have a long nose and sharp, pointed teeth.

slugs (SLUHGZ) Slimy, snail-like animals without shells that live mostly in forests, gardens, and damp places, and that feed on plants.

species (SPEE-sheez) A single kind of plant or animal. For example, all people are one species.

temperature (TEM-pruh-cher) How hot or cold something is.

venom (VEN-um) A poison passed by one animal into another through a bite or sting.

23

INDEX

WEB SITES

To learn more about garter snakes, check out these Web sites:

http://www.umass.edu/umext/snake/cgarter.html
http://www.mbnet.mb.ca/~smunro/snakes

24